The Secret to Start and Develop Your Own Business

Miquel Marvin Samuels

Maryland, USA

The Secret to Start and Develop Your Own Business

© 2009 by Miquel Marvin Samuels
All rights reserved.

ISBN : 9766108668
LCCN

Printed in the United States of America.

Introduction

I wrote this book as a guide to keep me grounded. This book is not about management, it does not teach about organisational structures. However it will show you how to start and develop your own business. You'll learn how to be successful in your own life by your creations. It is easy to read and is straight forward.

Learn how money really works and how to use your own resources to start and develop your own business. This book will give you results

Acknowledgements

I would like to thank all persons who encourage me to write this book.

Special thanks to my mother Beverly Lyseight and Mrs Marshall the vice principal of Bladensburg High School, for the motivation and support which they given me.

Contents

i	Introduction	
iii	Acknowledgements	
1	Finance / Support	1
2	Master the Secrets of Patience	4
3	Remember you Got a Life	8
4	Fear and Going in the Unknown	11
5	Biggest Secret is to Stay Focus	15
6	Motivation and De-motivation	19
7	Perseverance	23
8	Using your ideas to work for you	26
9	Finding Yourself and Products	29
10	The Relationship of Giving	33
11	Risks	36
12	The Payoff Reward	39

The Secret to Start and Develop Your Own Business

1

FINANCE / SUPPORT

When starting your own business you must have money, either your own money or borrowing someone else money. The money will allow you the freedom to set the most credential things a business need to start, such as materials, researches, development and traveling.

There are many financial levels to start from. Meaning you can have all the money to start or you can start from just using the skills you have acquired. If you are as passionate as I was to start your own business, you would start at any level life provided. I did not have any money; all I had were my ideas and dreams. This is the level that will test your strength to see if you have what it takes to start develop and manage a business. You will have to pull up your sleeves and decide to work extremely hard at this level. People are not so willing to give money. I am not saying that the world is so cold, or no one will help you; of course not, people are out there willing to help, but usually those people went through so much sacrifice and hardship to have what they desired. One would have to come with a very convincing business plan, which shows the lender would receive a big profit or interest.

If however you have the money to start your own business or have already develop the business. The smart thing to do is to use the money as a security to get a loan with the lowest interest rate possible; then make the business grow itself and pay its own expenses.

However if you have no money to start, a business, no form of education, just start! Start with your first idea, then go out there into the society and try to sell your idea. You might feel nervous to go out there by yourself; but you will find various kinds of people out there willing to give you advised. People are like angels. They will ensure that you are on the right path. "Continue", they would say. With that first step comes your first experience.

Using the first experience as an advantage step two will even get better. A sale may never come until days after. However with each step forward you are perfected. With every profit your business makes the business will grow. You must be your own boss. Your idea will manifest into a product. Then you'll have to market that product using samples. With the steps mentioned above find the purpose of the product!

Now your business has developed to a point. Some people bought your products and many more liked it, but argued it's too expensive. O.K. Fine! Remember people made your products better and it's them who will determine the value of the products. It's better to make small profits while sales are faster, then to get big profit with one sale.

SUPPORT

Support comes and goes just like the weather. It's difficult to show someone else the big picture you see. They do not understand the pain and how your body yearns for success. To gain support in what you believe in is important. Support coming from your family and a love one will make you balance.

FINANCE / SUPPORT

Support for me means knowing there is someone who cares and want to see me succeed; not necessarily someone to give me money, just someone to have trust in me. To know someone is there listening to my complaints and encouraging me. Not someone to discourage my dreams or say what they believed.

Unfortunately, support is hard to get, just as the finance to start a business. Do not worry; the secret to get support is to make it come to you. How? O.K.! It's like this; someone will test you to see if you have what it takes to start a business. That someone can be anyone interested in you. Saying for example you are willing to start a business because you know it's possible you can be more financially stable. If you do not show that you are determine and you will never quit the business. Investors will never support you.

If you honestly believe in your idea and product and the answers are yes O.K. there you go. The support comes best from you. It's better to depend on others than yourself; you can trust yourself to listen to the criticism of others to make you better. Love yourself and know that you are not alone spiritually. Do fitness to pass the time, be patient, eat good wholesome food and be clean and beautiful. Treat yourself special by going out to parties and being happy or even dining at a fine restaurant is a great idea. Satisfy your needs first. Always be calm in your spirit and allow that urge and pain which is inside of you to make you successful and progressive.

When you create a product others will see your true potential and then want to support your idea. Fortunate for me the experience in self-love and self support teaches me that emotion has no space in my business. The decisions you make are compromised when you are hurt and bitter. If you don't have any support, use the emotion of loneliness; to support yourself and be creative within your own time.

2

MASTER THE SECRETS OF PATIENCE

In this century the fast moving world of technology, the internet put a heavy burden on us to work faster; which leaves us with no time to do the little stuff, such as to smell a rose. When you lost energy because of working hard and fast, usually you become selfless. So, therefore your objective on what is important to you and the development of your business is critical. It will be harder to start your own business when you can not see the smaller parts of the picture. The biggest empire started from dirt to rocks. Everything in life as we know started from very little then grows to maturity. We are grown in a routine way of doing things. In order to be secure into today's society, we must work and usually that means working for someone else. I understand that when you have children in school, your utility bills and other bills must be paid, therefore to pay; you can't just leave your job to start your own business. In fact I will give you an example. I worked for a company for seven years, while I was there I gained experience in supervisory and enhance my qualification. This gave me more confidence. Yes of course I wanted more money when I was working for others, because like most of us we know our worth. But usually we will settle for what is offered to us. Anyway, I continued the job and worked toward my business.

It was a great thing to start my own business because I learned along the way, the art to be patient. I saw the big picture of the business I wanted, but didn't see the smaller picture, which is taking things step by step, moment by moment and to listen in order to make wise decisions. With these mistakes I was put to the test to see if I really wanted my own business. Having a job at the company made me felt secure. I got benefits and paid vacations. Most importantly I had an income. Now that I am on my own, I must go out there and make my own in Income.

I had two fears to deal with my ego and myself to master. I decided to make the business make itself from the beginning. As nervous as I was I went to the public to sell myself. It took a long time before I could see any progress. Determination is the advantage to learn to be patient. It's as if you can smell the pie how sweet it is, so you wait until it comes. I used that same approach to manifest my ideas into products. I also passed the test. I really wanted my own business, so I started anyway which eventually showed me to be patient. I am now one step ahead to accomplishing my goal. The secret to learn patient is to be slow in your approach while doing anything. Do not worry about the time eventually you will be done. It's so relaxing doing things slowly.

When you are patient you will see the details and at the end your energy will be speared. You will definitely get more done at the end of the day, and you and your own business will be profitable. Use the extra time to rest, love and think on ways to make your business better. Work on your ideas.

The Secret to Start and Develop Your Own Business

Have you ever cook on a very slow portable electric stove? Well try it sometime, because the best way to get tasty fried chicken is to keep the fried pot on the heat for about 15 minutes before the cooking oil is added into the pot. Then wait again for another 5 -10 minutes to make the cooking oil get hot enough to fry the chicken. Now the chicken must stay on one side for an additional 15 -20 minutes and on the other side for the same time. I hope you are remembering as you read. Note! When you have to get something done with no or limited resources, it is still possible to make it work for you.

I had no job, so I must buy my own food to cook. The way I could cook was with this very old broken electric stove. I used what I had and I ate eventually. I lived in conditions, which never came to me before for several years, because I believed in my business and myself.

Another example of patience is to be in a relationship. It is never easy to work or live with someone else. These are the same examples of life that can be used to practice patience. Listen to make wise decisions, use your eyes to see if someone may hurt you or your business. Notice with old people they do things slowly, not because they may be weak. It's because they are now being patient because of their health. Why do you think they make soldiers peal hundreds of potatoes in the military? It teaches patience. My favorite cousin Melloney witnessed that and told me.

Another way I learned to be patient is fitness, I practice fitness regularly. I ran cross-country in high school and I continued running throughout my life. I fined it to be a patient sport. It clears my mind from everything when I run. One step follows the other step until I achieved my goal when I run. All the organs in your body are breathing. The heart, stomach, muscles and the blood in my body are so warm. Usually when I finish running my brain feels so relaxed, fresh and rested. It's

MASTER THE SECRETS OF PATIENCE

like I am new again. The key is that jogging is a very patient activity. You must have a determination to reach the finish line without stopping.

If something goes wrong or someone hurt your feeling, try very hard to put it aside. It's not important to yourself and your business. BE PATIENT AND CAREFUL.

3

REMEMBER YOU - GOT A LIFE TOO

Learn to be patient and that's the start. You already know you are the driving force for your own business finance and support. You know if you are patient you will accomplish; Great Things.

My mother told me I should take care of number one. At first I thought that was selfish of her to tell me such a thing. But over time I came to know what she really meant. Make sure your immediate needs are met. Your emotion is important to you not your business. You need emotion to live fully. However there is a way that can give you love and emotion; if you have no support. First, look at life has it is, which is to live and be amongst the living. Do so by socializing with others. It's good for your skills and to develop your own business. The responsibility of life is demanding. We must pay attention to various aspects of our lives.

Let's start by highlighting the many areas of our lives and how important it is to satisfy your needs. The body, mind and soul have to be taken care of by you. Make sure your skin is always fresh and clean. Go to beach occasionally. Stretch your body whenever any time you feel like. Touch your toes and reach for the sky. Take a deep breath (inhale) hold it for a minute and then exhale. It make your brain feels light. Keep your mind free from all negative thoughts. Think about the future of your business. Find a way to be balance.

The same mother who told me to worry about number one, asked me what I mean by been balance. Well to be balance is to satisfy every needed area of your body, mind and soul. The mind gives us the biggest challenge, just because it is the area of the unknown. There are two ways to use the mind at your advantage, we use our mind to learn and analyze things? Be wise and certain about your decision making. Don't worry about anything. Have no fear; believe in yourself. Allow the intuition to work; it will guide you to your destiny. What we have in our minds are usually what we adapted from our childhood. Avoid negative thoughts, think positive and allow your mind. You would have to change this negative energy to positive force. Use the mind to love yourself and people.

The positive force in your mind will help you to appreciate life. Then you'll surely get up every day and do the things that will make you better. Go out at night's party until tomorrow. Make love and have fun; just be safe. One thing I will say about the creator is that he gave us wisdom knowledge and understanding. He allows us to make our own choices. Just be honest about it.

We need the air, water, sunlight and food in order to live. So it is our responsibility to take care of them too. Animals are just like us; it's just that they communicate differently. We need to be kind to them. You see, it's important that you are healthy in all aspect of your life, because when your own business is established as a company or even an empire. You need to be alive

The Secret to Start and Develop Your Own Business

and health long enough to enjoy your accomplishment and to see the legacy lives on. So while you are young, live life to the fullest. Do not hurt anyone include yourself; it will only break you down in the long run. Free your mind and allow the extra energy to do all the work. Your greater love will comes later, the family.

4

FEAR AND GOING INTO THE UNKNOWN

I used this topic because all of us are naturally fearful. Unfortunately fear and business do not mix; it's like putting water with oil. We are limited to what are known as people and that's fearful to us. We examined the different forces of mankind and are fearful of the wars. We were taught how to work and pay the bills. I never went to a distinguished University. But I often wondered if these schools are isolated special schools for wealthy families to rule the world. I believe most of us are the under dogs. It's very hard to work from the bottom up to build your own life and a business. But it's possible. So we work for others who are already wealthy. You must know this; every wealthy family today was once poor. Someone in their family had a dream using their ideas and make empire for their family to prosper. Family unity started at the beginning of time. The family that masters the secrets of togetherness allowed their generation to be prosperous today. For example look at one very popular family and history in the world such as Queen of England. They made sure their family stayed together and indeed they grow throughout the centuries.

This is to show you how, intimidating it is to start your own business. No one wants to start a business and a few years down the line it collapsed. That is why they say the fittest of the fittest will survive. That is why you must be perfect in your approach to start your own business.

Now the best way to face fear is to deal with it. Meaning if you fear something, you must first know the reasoning for the fear. The only way you can know is to face the fear itself, know that fear can not hurt you. It's you who will end up hurting yourself. Here are some examples. Imagine it's a beautiful sunny day and you are walking alone in the park. There are some children playing football a distance ahead and not too far away a couple walking together holding hands. Ha! You feel good for the birds are flying and singing melody in your ears. While you walked down the path you noticed a man walking fast towards you? Naturally your heart starts to beat fast, because you are wondering if this man will hurt you. You try to look calm, but you taught in your mind that he is a killer. When you are afraid of someone fear shows on you; so fear in itself, signifies that I am afraid. So you panics and the man walked pass and even said hello. See you put your self through unnecessary stress, because you allowed the fear to torment your mind and body. I am not saying you should not be alert. Just trust yourself to make the right decision and allow your intuition to guide you. There are many ways, to conquer your fear. With the story about the park, just to say the man was indeed a killer. By not been fearful, the alertness would make you fight back the killer or maybe you would run.

People who live in areas where violence is prevalent tend to be fearful of every thing and everybody. Surprise, that's all intimidation in your mind. I am a believer in the saying, what goes around comes around. The definition in the form of people

FEAR AND GOING INTO THE UNKNOWN

is if you are involved in violence or any wrong doings, you will end up paying the price later for your action.

So you need to know that fear will hold you back. Start your own business and master the self secrets. Know that you must look your own resources and sale for your business. Often time fear will come over you. It happens to me too that's how I can talk about it. No one was interesting in buying my products. When I went into the first store the security at the door would not let me in much less to allow me to talk to the manager. The security asked me if I had an appointment. O.K. just to say I got through. The next barrier is the workers saying no the manager is not interested. It seems to me that the workers were jealous. If you proceed persist you may get to talk to the purchasing manager. If your products are creative the manager will say so. But maybe the store has it own challenges dealing with at that time, so they refuse to buy at that time. Yes! Maybe you will not get a sale the first time but the best thing to do is persevere, at some point some one will consider buying your product. When you try to develop a product, and you don't have money; it will be hard work in the beginning. Do not let the fear stop you from going to another store. The stores will teach, and show you what you're doing wrong because they are very critical. Understand that the stores must be critical because they have a business to operate.

One of the most important tools to use against fear is to be confident. Be ready to respond to your company competently. Dress formal, be good, feel great and believe in yourself; and the products. Be very opened minded. Listen to everything. Remember what I said about emotions, it's not good for your business. I put going into the unknown next to fear because at the point when people are being critical they tells you what they like, because they are the ones who will purchase the product. Some people will set out to discourage you but you should be wise to differentiate the intention and simply walk away. Now you know that fear wouldn't hurt the unknown. The experience of stopping on the corner where the thugs are and knowing they are human? They are just like you. Maybe one of them might give you an advice that would make your business successful. Try to be wise with the difference of personalities, and allow yourself the opportunities for the success of your own business.

5

BIGGEST SECRET IS TO STAY FOCUS

To stay focus, I required you to be knowledgeable and alert about every movement you make with those you will encounter. Know your product inside and out, have timely goals and be effective. At this point in your business you should be stable. Meaning your business should be organized and at a location, which can be your home. Put everything your business is using in categories by function and use. Save the important things and throw out the trash/garbage. There are two main distractions noise and people. If your location is amongst people practice to tone down. Do you remember when you had homework to do as a teenager? You would be playing the music as well as watching the television at the same time. When I am working on something or even reading a book, I am listening, I am hearing everything that is been said on the television with out even looking on it. I figured out that women are very good listeners. They also can do many things at once; I started to notice the actions of women with my mother and grandmothers. They would get a lot of their demands met. At first I did not notice how they would analyze things automatically until I was fully on my own. Actually when I started my business it was very hard to cope with myself and my needs. I used my grandmother surviving skills to my advantage. I would go around her regularly and did any thing she wanted, such as hang up clean curtains on the windows and worked in the back yard. I was giving her my helping hand knowing that I was learning from her will and strength. She was so willing to tell me everything about what I should not do and how I must be secure. She would say, "If you can't be good be careful." Do what you are supposed to and do not cry. It seems she was testing my manhood. Deep down I could see she wanted me to accomplish a lot, but she never told me what to accomplish. The point is that I adopted a lot of her female intuition and powers. The greatest thing about her is that she was very stern.

Noise can drive some of us mad. I moved to a neighborhood where the dogs were noisy and loud. When the people get off the streets say about 9-10 p.m. That's when figuratively 100 dogs come out to start a debate about area borders and female bitches. Anyway I learned to channel all my thoughts to what ever I am doing; even if I am trying to get some sleep. I try not to have any emotional feelings about events I have no control over. People call it denial. After a while you don't even notice that noise as important anymore.

If you do not have someone to support you personally, you can get depressed because sometimes we need someone to balance us. It is at this point you should use your time wisely. Take a break and do something else. If you need emotional support by all means satisfy yourself. Then come back to your work, you'll find that you are more focus at that time. Sometimes no matter what everything seems to be going wrong, the equipment is malfunctioning and one problem follows another, and on top of that you have a dead line to meet and you don't feel so good. In a sense you just feel like giving up. Do not give up. Stop and think about how to take different approaches. Dissect everything with a magnified glass. Be patient and calm, do not panic. Start over your work if you have to. Do what ever it takes to get the work done. To finish is the priority, not to be upset. Remember there is on space for emotions in your business, all you want is a solution. Take a break go eat some food and make sure you are fine. If you are tired go to sleep, you can continue another time. The solution for your problems will be solved by you eventually. The secret is to persevere; because perseverance is always testing our faith. "Do you really want to achieve your goal?" perseverance will say.

Having a family of your own is very demanding on the parents, much less one parent. Children can be a hand full for you. Sometime to find time to eat is impossible. That's why I strongly believe young people should organize their life the way they want, before they start their family. Your family will require a great deal of your time. You can still try to start your own business with the intention that your family will know what your ambitions are and will be willing to support you. Even then you must be focus, do not allow them to distract you at work. Friends will require your friendship. You can do thing with them, you must be balance. You must monitor your time very well. The business is important to you. Your family and friends will benefit later when you achieve. If you're working temporarily and you start your own business it can be a problem after a while because your business will demand a lot of your time. When I worked for this organization and wanted to go on the road, all I did was make sure no one wasn't waiting for me nor looking for me. So I would use that time to go on the road to do my personal business and stayed longer than my lunchtime.

While working for this other company I was very ambitious to start my own business, having no time for the business. I put my trust into a lot of people I did not even know fully. I allowed them to handle my money and transactions for me; when I should be doing it myself. There are good people; but

The Secret to Start and Develop Your Own Business

people will think how to benefit from your money. I found myself firing and hiring regularly. That's not a healthy style in developing your own business.

6

MOTIVATION *AND* DE-MOTIVATION

First of all you must have a natural drive to see your business establish. You should possess that natural motivation to be independent, financially stable and having the desire to help others. Motivation is a tool that will empower you to your goals. When the goals are achieved then you'll get to accomplish the ultimate goals, which is to have your own business.

Motivation in itself encourages you to start taking action to each goal or idea. It gives you the energy to use your physical power to start doing things to achieve your goal. Some people use the example of others to their goal. You need to know that motivation guaranteed NO promises. It has no power by itself. It's not alive, it can not act alone. Remembered you can only use the pattern of someone else approach to motivate and accomplish your goals. It's the perseverance that helps you to go on, even when your plans are not manifesting it self. What I am saying, is with your own unique ideas you can use your intuition to guide your approach in reaching your goal. Believe in your powers, it is there to help and guide you.

There is another way to motivate; people can use sorrows to motivate them to act. They will use that type of pain to motivate them to act toward achieving their goals. Maybe the routine started when they were children and their parents physically forced them to do things. The child will resist usually, but still must obey. So! Overtime the child will depend on that forceful approach to achieve their goal. I personally believe to feel sorry for yourself is not healthy. The personality to adopt, to deal with problems and depression; must be forceful. That is why people are in jail.

Motivation encourages us by ways of defense. If we are about to loose a car or house, that fact in itself will force you to do things which you would not normally do in order not to loose that car or house. The various countries in the world uses defense to motivate them to go to war. People do the same thing too.

Usually when a love one or even a good friend die it motivates you to start acting on your plan which you considered years ago to start your own business, buy a house or a car, get married, have children, leave your dead beat job and to do what you always wanted. That is a sad way to motivate you, but it encourages us to act very strongly towards our goal.

And the strongest force of motivation is happiness. YES! Happy it is and Joyful when a couple is expecting a child and when that baby is born. It motivates them to act and plan for the baby's arrival. The pageant mother kept her appointment with the doctor and does all the necessary preparation to ensure that she carry a healthy child, while the father prepares a safe environments and shelter for the arrival of the child. Now that a new baby is coming it motivates the father to do thing to make the mother happy. When you accomplish a good plan for your business; that joy of achievement will motivate you to take the next action with more encouragement. If for so long you have

MOTIVATION *AND* DE-MOTIVATION

been trying, believe in your plans and persevere. You have been standing strong against the power of de-motivation, and family disbelief in you. Finally your product sold off and gave you big profits and something good happen to you with your idea or plans. That accomplishment will motivate you to believe and go on.

De-motivation will take the power from motivation if you allow it. De-motivation can make weak persons want to kill themselves. De-motivation allows you to make negative and bad things happen to your business and your regular life. It destroys anything it gets in contact with, it sadden the soul and heart. It will make you feel sick and then you get sick. It depresses the body for you not to act toward your goals, only if you allow the force of de-motivation to take the place of motivation. They will not be friends and they cannot be friends; only when a love one dies.

You believe to yourself that you are always creative, very easy to learn and you always do a great job working for someone else. Not accomplishing the things you want such as a car, house, clothes and furniture and all this happen because you do not plan. But deep down inside your soul, heart, body and mind you know that you should or must be independent totally. You must have your own business; yet you are very secure in a well paid job. You are de-motivated to act on starting and developing your own business, because you may have responsibilities such as rent/mortgage, utility bills, food and your children to take care of. De-motivated because there is no money in the bank not even to start a business or capitalize on your plans and ideas.

O.K., I understand the risks one will take to start their business in this situation. My Uncle took the same risks while he had a wife, four children, a house and a car, every single thing for his family's comfort. He decided to use this get rich lesson program he saw on the television to start his own business. The lessons were how to manage buy and sell real estate. He left his job and used his own savings with mortgages to buy properties. Then he repairs them and rent the houses to people. Very good for my uncle, he was de-motivated for years then got motivated to start. But my uncle failed just because his wife de-motivated his motivation to see and fight through the problems; and most importantly to believe in his plans, ideas and goals to have his own business. In the end his wife lifts him and took the children. The tenants in the houses were not paying their rents. So he could not pay for loan on his mortgage and so the bank took the properties from them eventually.

For years he had it very hard with depression, loneliness and failure. Years past and he got a job at his previous work place. I bet he was blaming his failure on trying to start his own business. NO! It is not the business that caused his failure, I believe that's a deeper power of de-motivation got him. I will say keep focus on the plan, the goal and believe in your ideas.

This other area of de-motivation is when you found out that the one who loves you the most such as your mother and siblings gets jealous of you. They noticed how you are focus and motivated to accomplishing your goals. The business has reach a level of comfort, Yet they don't feel or want to be apart of your achievements. The way to deal with the situation is to leave it alone. They will come around. You must know that de-motivation is very powerful; it will weaken the will to achieve; it's here, there and everywhere. De-motivation is alive while motivation must be use by you to benefit yours needs. Use your motivational skills to make de-motivation have no place in your plans and ideas while starting and developing your own business. Sometime you will feel as if you just cannot go on any further. Do not make de-motivation win. You must and will win.

PERSEVERANCE

The key tools in accomplishing your own business are persistence and perseverance, this is where most developing business will fail. Every business will encounter problems and difficulties. Sometimes natural disaster such, as flood, earthquake, hurricane such delight, can hurt your business place. That's why there are insurance. It will be unfortunate if for some financial reason you do not get insured. The decisions you make is very important for your business development.

The area of perseverance that will help your business is you. You'll push to get the things that will benefit the business. Keep up the strength, make your believe alive and make it grow. Would you give up on your own child? Of course not! The child needs your perseverance to let him/her grow up until he/she become an adult, and can manage on his/her own. If that same approach don't work do not give up continue until you succeed.

The Secret to Start and Develop Your Own Business

Be sure the other areas of the business are planned carefully for the interest of the business. If there is a product to introduce into the market and you tried everything to sell that product. But it's putting a financial burden on the business. It's very easy to want to give up when you first start but you must give continuing attends to make it work. Don't give up! When a creation is new it is very difficult to get people to accept it. Companies with money use their finances with commercial television to promote a new product; making the market out there feels as if they know the product. The better job the marketing staff do to introduce the product, the better response the product gets.

If there is little or no money to market your product, use the resource that is available to you. You are the biggest resources to use on getting a product to sell. First plan your approach carefully. Use the many channels of communication to introduce your product. Make a list of the stores and places you'll ask to sell your product. Use the newspaper to advertise the product and print fliers too. Call the marketing company and set appointment to show them your products. Please be professional because they have the power to make a difference in sales for you. They know the market well. It is a must that you work hard and long until there is a way you can follow.

Another way to introduce a new product is to enter contest. Do your research, look and find a way to do some publication for your products. You can go to radio station and media houses. Work out something with them, communicate effectively with these people. Walk from door to door call people tell them about your products. The important tool to use when selling is to make the person feel welcome and comfortable. Use good words to comfort and charming words to welcome them. Please dress appropriately like a professional person. Make sure you are health and fit. You'll need all the energy to persevere, take sometime to rest and energize yourself.

PERSEVERANCE

Experiment and perseverance means infinite love and believe towards your new product and your own business. Accept when a product or the business fail. I accept failure when the situation proved not to be a challenge. Sometimes it's not the right timing. Once I had a new product in many stores for over one year before it became popular, like hot bread. People follow each other so if one person buys your product others will follow. It is very important to be patient, especially when we are communicating with people to accept your product.

I hope with this example you'll know that perseverance is a natural part of life. One day I was thinking heavily on how I was progressing in my business. I was at my friend's mini market shop, where I go regularly for comfort. June and Rodney with their children are very good friends to me. While I sat on the chair looking around that day, I noticed a stream of water along the street running towards the sea. The rain fell earlier and hit a yellow leaf from a very green tree into the stream. Being that the shop was not too far from the sea. The breeze was blowing heavily. So the leaf went down the stream and hit a rock that was out of the water. Then the breeze brews the leaf back even further than where it initially started.

The leaf persevered to get to the sea in different ways, but there was many barriers to set the leaf back. Imagine the distance to the sea and the many barriers that will be in the leaf way. I looked for a long time until I didn't even realized when I stopped looking. I looked again and the leaf got further down the stream until it was gone. To persevere is a fight and struggle so keep up and eat pie at the end.

USING YOUR IDEAS TO WORK FOR YOU

If you are the type of person who is constantly thinking on ways to be rich? Not only that, but good ideas plague you like, a mystique in your ear. You can't dismiss it unless something is done to stop the problem.

Notice children when an idea comes to them. They wouldn't even think twice not to act. We did things so freely, then learn ways that will work or not. So you would learn by your mistakes the proper approach to take the next time. Now that you are older, you tent to stop yourself from acting in the future, mainly because of fear. Don't you think the ideas come to you for a reason? Idea are not teacher or given to you by someone. It usually comes natural. It must be that same greater force out there guiding us on what to do and how to make the right decisions, the decisions to benefit you in the future.

We tend not to follow that particular direction. We always chose the side that will hurt and make us work harder. We

USING YOUR IDEAS TO WORK FOR YOU

at times travel the longest way, just because our nature is stubborn. For someone to be successful in starting and developing your own business they must learn how to use their intuition. In earlier times men did not know how to translate intuition into lessons, because man and scientist could not figure out how to apply intuition to everyday life. Kings and legion used intuition to direct their life and others too. They often have a god of inspiration to their powers. In today's century we are benefiting globally from people who used their intuition and follow their ideas. Now we have the computer and many other things which were before such as the telephone, television, cars, cloths, watches, process food, air craft and the list goes on. If those people didn't follow their intuition and take action towards their idea, we would not be enjoying a better life today. Who knows, maybe if more people had followed their intuition, situation would be far better than it is now. Individual ideas are stolen for one man's benefit. But to be wealthy you must take on your own challenge. Sometimes you need to approach the situation or idea differently! This may requires you to gain more knowledge. The key is not to give up easily.

Now we know that when an intuition gives us an idea the best thing to do is to act on it. If your idea is to create or invent a new product, that comes through your intuition. The first step to take is to figure out how you will make this idea a reality. Start using your knowledge wisely to put ideas together. Use people to find out what ever you need to know, in order to develop your idea. Intuition encourages results. If you make the first step intuition will show you the next step. Ideas can come in different form. The persons who are capable of fulfilling and nurturing these ideas are as real life maybe you will become a famous write in your younger stage of life. The idea came to you, the title of a book and its' content. You took the action, went through with perseverance, wrote the book and published it. Say we look in a crystal ball to the future and you are the best seller in it's time. I am sure you would be happy to have taken the action then. What if you were to become very rich in 20 years and you are now 12 years old. The plans for your life would probably be to complete high school, have fun for 2 years, (can you make your imagination run wild by thing about the word fun). Working for a bank as an accountant for 4 years; then loose your job. Can you imagine loosing all your assets which you have worked long and hard to achieve? Not having a job to sustain you. Then you are force to use your idea which will make you wealth in 5 to 8 years. The idea is that you will create this product which will be popular with in a specific period. First you will act and develop the idea of the product, then under go all the pains and rejections. Some what like the woolla whop success story. The idea continue itself by telling you to go door, stand on the corner in the town and beg people to try out the product and buy it. You worked for many years, until faith presents itself. Finally you get a break through by selling billions of your products because it became the main item of use to the people. Then you become filthy rich.

If you are already working to develop your own business, it's very important that you understand the importance of acting on the intuition of ideas. I believe every idea that comes is valuable to you and society, so do not ignore them. At some point in your life you must take action. If not you will pay the price for been neglectful. So far in history no body was wrong, if someone didn't succeed. It's because they gave up on the challenge which plagued them. That's failing. Persons will live for the rest of their lives working hard for others; if stressful life style doesn't kill them early.

FINDING YOURSELF AND PRODUCTS

When an idea is becomes a product the relationship you'll have with it will be infinite love. Even when you die, the legacy will live on. If your ideas created something looking futuristic and your mind tells you it will surely fail. Then you will become more hesitant to act on your idea. Yet you are so comfort and secure with your job, but still miserable because you're not being yourself at work.

Most of us are working for someone else. With that choice we limit ourselves to receive what is intended for our happiness. Our world is industrialized to benefit the people who are already rich. So it will be harder for us to take a piece of the pie. It is possible to be financially free. It's harder now because our family didn't fulfill their ideas or dreams. Our generation that was in the past was weak. They said my children will do what I did not. That is why our generation is facing difficult challenges at this level across the world.

Whatever financial level life presents to you, from the most difficult challenge to the easiest one you must start finding yourself and purpose on earth. Start by using the intuition to create unique and different product or idea. Use the human skill to guide you to your destiny. Guaranteed! When you take chances in life you'll see that, they will work for you in the further. Now you'll feel like you have a purpose on earth. That motivation will make you persist to the end of race.

While creating a new product or allowing your intuition to work and develop an idea, you'll find compassion in your heart and feel alive. You'll know that you don't have to follow anyone's way of doing things to secure yourself. You are a unique person find the strength and trust the intuition to be your own person.

The world around us is institutionalizing us to believe it's a pattern. It seems like we must follow this concept to be successful on earth. Policies are made in such a way that we are dependent on their uses to live. Technology has it benefits when used of course. But the point is when you can not afford the product you are lift behind.

Put yourself in a financial freedom by acting now on your intuition and develop your business. Be in-dependent. You'll never be lift behind again. Do not let fear control your powers to act. In this book I promote self independence. However I want to use this example to make working professionals or someone who is working for a company knows the truth. Some people inspiration is for just the simplest things in life, such as, motherhood. Whereby some people are inspired to be lawyers, doctors and so on. Using their intuition they will persevere and accomplish their goal. Professional persons, such as doctors, lawyers and business owner are comfortable in their jobs.

FINDING YOURSELF AND PRODUCTS

While I was pursuing my idea to start and develop my own business, many ideas came to me after the first one. Even when I produce a product which I was certain that the design was finished, then I realized it was not completed. Initially I have made the designs to go on the note books, but I end up putting it on a t-shirt instead. That change motivated me to do other designs for the note books as well as the T-shirts. I found myself thinking the first idea was the product. Because I took the first step I found my product and myself taking another step which was; something different.

You can never know what is in store for you. The products you will create can make a profound difference in people's life. The reward will be yours. Do not think you are working for money only. You will never make it with greed. Know that in some way you will make someone happy out there. People that will work for you will benefit greatly as well, because you are a creator. So know you'll be changing and helping life for the best time to come.

Once, I designed some beautiful framed items. Written inside the framed item was a beautiful poem laid beside a beautiful floral blouse. The pharmacy bought them by the dozen. It was the type of product to make a difference in profit; the few stores selling the product must sell a lot. Like a thousand are more.

I took up the challenge for the first time and went on the streets to sell. Mark you, I know just a little about selling. So I began to sell, I was very energetic ready to get people to buy my products. The people walked pass me as if I wasn't even there. They would look on the products because they were different. The vibrant energy I had got low, "Look beautiful frames for your bathroom and bedroom. Come buy," I said. Not getting a sale I put the products on a box and stopped shouting. Minutes after people stopped and enquired about my products.

The product showed me how to allow this new creation to sell it. I learnt how to make the products affordable when I first started marketing them. People like good things and new product too. But some people are very cautious as to how they welcome new comers. It is fine when people are just being themselves. However, I sold off all the products in three hours. This motivated me to go out there again. My products defined me and made themselves available to people.

Also when I write a literature the intuition flows freely than when I write a poem. For with the poem I would go back and change the words to give the poem more rhythm, flavor and emotion. Allow your intuition to be free, carve your life's future and generation too.

10

CHAPTER TITLE

THE RELATIONSHIP OF GIVING

The relationship of giving is blessing to you, the creation and the development of your own business, which will help us all. You are not the world's mother or father; neither should you give to every one around you. Give when a person is in need and when you can, even if it's the last. Never mine! Before you know it you'll have the giving spirit.

Sometimes you will feel like giving for no reason, by all means do so. Just be careful, people will lie to make you give to them. If this is the case don't worry because they will have that sin to live with.

People give to benefit. For example if you buy an item, you will get one free; making the customer spend more money than they intend to spend. My mother is a woman that is always giving. People would come by the house with their one child or children begging for something. They would ask for small things like salt, black pepper, onion, butter and other things that are necessary for living. I believe because my mother gave so much, our family was always blessed. We were never in need.

The Secret to Start and Develop Your Own Business

When my mother standard of living improved she began giving in abundance without hesitation. My mother wasn't a rich woman. She was only rich in her heart. Although her emotion was broken in many ways, she succeeded.

To ask for something is as important as to give. Mother never teaches me to ask for things. Fortunate for me I first learnt to beg when I was a child at school. We begged each other for things all the time. Children were friendly, so begging was easy, it seems normal to us then. When I was a child I would spend all of my money and would not have any bus fare to get home. I played games and slot machines after school hoping to win some money, but ending up losing all my money. I must still get home so I would beg persons for bus fare. Sometimes the ladies would say where is your fare? COME! Grab my hands and carry me on the bus with them and paid my fare. If nothing worked I would go on the bus head straight to the back, hoping that the bus would reach my stop before the conductor gets to me. Even though I went to the back of the bus the conductor would get to me before I reached my stop. Then he would asked, "Where is your bus fare?" and I would always say nothing until I get off.

The point of this story is no matter what it takes, I reached my destination. Rodney from the same shop told me in my older stage in life "when I was developing my business I had little or no money." He said, "when ever you are in need of something don't be afraid to ask, for it, the answer can only be yes or no; and what if the answer is yes. He also said a good friend is better than a good plate of food; meaning it's good to share than to be all for yourself.

What he told me was so true because many times I have no money and I have important things to be done. I would go out there and something would always workout. I communicate very well so that people will accept my plea. I never thought that I would have mentioned the act of asking to you, but when I think on the topic giving I realized that asking and giving is parallel. To give and ask must be a regular part of your life; it will help you to build a relationship with others. Let's go back into history. People would share their labor with each other. For example the man who lives on the hill is a builder; beside him lives a farmer and most of the people in the community had a skill. So they gave and asked each other for help. This was done for or the betterment of the community. No money was needed then. Nature gives and received all the time. The trees give to the sun, people and the earth. While the sun gives to the people and living things on earth.

11

RISKS

This book encouraged you to take risk because it is in the risks you'll find the magic. It is important for me to highlight the areas of risks.

While growing up all the risks I took always came through, having me thinking I can change things to the betterment of us all. While I worked for the one major company, I took risks with my job all the time. Sometimes I take risk to get a task complete. It is as if I can see the results before and while I am acting towards the results, or maybe it just hoping the risk would work.

Why I always get good results when I take a risk, is because I used all the skills I know to finalize a decision. It is knowledge that made me confident when I take a rest on the Job, it's because I know the manager is far away. In the back of my head I am always making decision for the interest of the company. However when I opted to start my own business, I used the same approach on how I took risks. That proved to be a challenge to my own business's development. The risk I took didn't always work in my favor. I learned by my own mistakes. When I did not have any money to take the risk, I used myself to get by. I did not receive a reward. But I learned of course, the hard way.

I believe in perseverance because you will get some results eventually. Taking risk is as if you are gambling with the money you already created. You will lose money that you worked really hard to get for your business. Knowledge is the way to take risks, know about what you are going in to.

For example, I really want a store for my business, mainly because my clients would ask me, where is this place? I presented the company I was developing as one that was already developed. I was very egoistic to get a location to be truthful to my clients and to have a place where people would come and sit and be comfortable to do business. I was the salesman, production manager, accountant and marketing manager for my company because I could not afford to employ any staff.

I eventually got a place. It had a few faults, but I arranged it to my comfort. The shop was in a small plaza with 15 other shops. It had another occupant, who was very unprofessional, I thought I could make a positive impact on her life, but sorry to say I did not. One day I simply asked her to remove the dirty mop from the entrance of the building.

Two months I officially opened my store. She became very aggressive, embarrassing, and disrespectful thus influencing my decision to leave the premises. After leaving this location I realized that the decision I have made to open this store at that point in time was not a wise one. However, I learned from my mistake and I continued my journey which is the journey to success. Take risk if you can afford to it may be rewarding at the end. Be knowledgeable about your own risks and your own business which you are developing.

12

THE PAY OFF REWARD

Use all the nature skills you are born with and create new and useful things to reward your future. Most people die not knowing their true potential. Some never allow the creation in them to shine; they chained themselves to fulfilling others ideas or dreams. Please be sure to act on the ideas and create the true life for you. Money was made for the purpose of collection, to take from you the creation of your bean. It is apart of our life some would say, but it can have positive or negative effect on our lives.

Fear is one of our greatest enemies that can destroy our inner strength. It is de-motivating factors that can create havoc in our everyday life. However we can overcome. The will to persevere and persist will help to build the morale standard of your business. It will make that vision or dream that you have longed waited for comes through. That is making the impossible possible. You might think that having one million dollars would be all good. All the riches in the world will not make you happy if it's not yours.

When I decided to start my own business I had no money. I tried every hard to get a loan in many ways. I tried the bank, my family, my friends and personal investors to invest in my idea. Nothing came through, however I kept the faith. I used the only resources I had, which was my skills and my dreams. I believed that the time I used working for others, should be used to develop my own business. I learned to be more responsible with my business and finances. Many times situation presents itself in a negative way for me to get money. The temptation was strong and I wanted to see the business developed. No one would want to go through years of pains, perseverance, persistent and broken dreams.

Money that comes too easy goes very easy. When families inherit riches, that blood money often pierces the hearts and minds of the inheritors and they lose everything in the end. Most time to be rich you would have created a product or manifested an idea, so if you die the legacy will live on. I have always said I don't want any thing free. I am willing to work as hard as it takes to get what I want. The bigger the dream the harder you will drive yourself. Remember if you hit someone the consequence for that will set you back. But not out of the race.

Money will always test your faith. The money is not important; the money is not real life. It's a paper! Control by the banks and wealthy people. Money is powerful because it's universal. If you use money to do well, wealth will be your reward. Where by if you use money to hurt, even yourself. You will lose it, do not use money for your own benefit help others too. If we were in the centuries when money was not created we would have used our trade or skill, if not we would have surely died.

Money circulates through all people. On day I took a bus and gave the bus conductor a coin, the coin had a special color painted on it. I totally forgot about that coin. Until days after I

The Secret to Start and Develop Your Own Business

took another bus and got back the same coin with the special paint on it. I remembered the paint because I used that coin to open the paint can. The paint was a special color. So, indeed money goes around and around.

Money will distract your creativity. When you are rich it made you free to buy the best things in life. BE FREE TO LIVE HAPPILY. This is the place in life all of us will love to be, unfortunately it is not going to come easy. Wealthy people created the life style they have by acting on their intuitions. The rich life style is a reward for being creative. Just as you see in society. The wealthy is always happy with their money, only because they understand the development of its being. They use money to buy things to make them comfortable and fulfilled their dreams by purchasing cars and a mansion on the mountain side.

To gain the world and have no one to share the riches with, will make you feel just like the materialize things you have; lifeless! While your own business is developing do everything in your power, be sincere, loving, giving and understanding. Please adapt the good communication skills. Your personality should reflect the multiple shades of soft golden lights coming up through the many channels to its creation. When you see that act you will want to touch and hold it forever. "It's your personality that holds the money." O.k. yes! The money will make you feel good. You will feel powerful to control people for your own benefit. Buying everything you want, or don't want only because you can. If you are not careful your money can be harmful. The choice is yours. The intuition can help you, "only if you look to its power for your guidance." Or you can fall to the negative energies. It's de-motivation. No! You don't want to be sad. Please be happy and create your own money.

www.ingramcontent.com/pod-product-compliance
Lightning Source LLC
LaVergne TN
LVHW051204080426
835508LV00021B/2805